D1466318

EUROPE

Troll Associates

EUROPE

by Rae Bains
Illustrated by Allan Eitzen

Troll Associates

Library of Congress Cataloging in Publication Data

Bains, Rae.
    Europe.

    Summary: Introduces some basic facts about the
European continent.
    1. Europe—Description and travel—1971-   —
Juvenile literature. [1. Europe] I. Eitzen, Allan, ill.
II. Title.
D923.B35   1985   940.55   84-8598
ISBN 0-8167-0304-3 (lib. bdg.)
ISBN 0-8167-0305-1 (pbk.)

Copyright © 1985 by Troll Associates, Mahwah, New Jersey
All rights reserved. No part of this book may be used
or reproduced in any manner whatsoever without written
permission from the publisher.
Printed in the United States of America

10 9 8 7 6 5 4 3 2 1

Invincible Roman legions march north, conquering every tribe in their path. Armored knights on horseback thunder toward one another in a medieval jousting tournament. King Arthur and Queen Guinevere sit at their court in the kingdom of Camelot. Robin Hood meets with his merry men in Sherwood Forest. And Joan of Arc, sword held high, leads the French army on to victory.

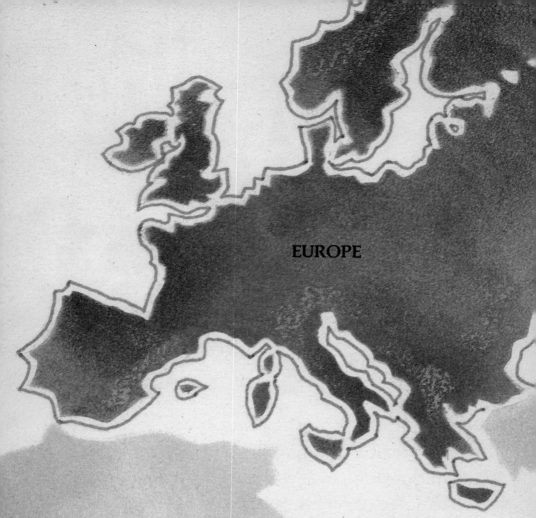

EUROPE

All of these people, places, and events seem as real to us as what we read in today's newspaper. Yet they are not images of here and now, but of another time and another place. The time is the past, and the place— rich in history and legend—is the continent of Europe.

ASIA

Of the world's continents only Australia is smaller than Europe. But in spite of its small size, Europe has a large population. And throughout history, Europeans have made important contributions to science, art, literature, music, architecture, and political thought.

Even though Europe is called a continent, it is actually part of a huge land mass known as Eurasia. Europe forms the smaller, western portion of Eurasia, while the larger, eastern portion is known as Asia.

At its western border, Europe is washed by the Atlantic Ocean, the North Sea, and the Norwegian Sea. To the north is the Barents Sea, which reaches up into the frigid Arctic Ocean. Along the southern edge of Europe are the warm waters of the Mediterranean Sea, the Adriatic Sea, the Aegean Sea, and the Black Sea.

At its eastern edge, Europe is separated from Asia by a long chain of mountains called the Urals. The Urals run north and south through the Soviet Union. The eastern part of the Soviet Union is in Asia, while the western part is in Europe.

At its western border, Europe is washed by the Atlantic Ocean, the North Sea, and the Norwegian Sea. To the north is the Barents Sea, which reaches up into the frigid Arctic Ocean. Along the southern edge of Europe are the warm waters of the Mediterranean Sea, the Adriatic Sea, the Aegean Sea, and the Black Sea.

At its eastern edge, Europe is separated from Asia by a long chain of mountains called the Urals. The Urals run north and south through the Soviet Union. The eastern part of the Soviet Union is in Asia, while the western part is in Europe.

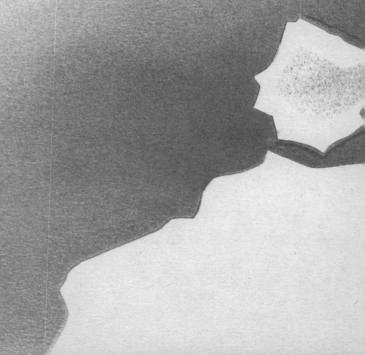

Besides the Soviet Union, there are thirty-two other countries in Europe. Natural barriers help separate some of them. For example, the Pyrenees Mountains form a natural border between France and Spain.

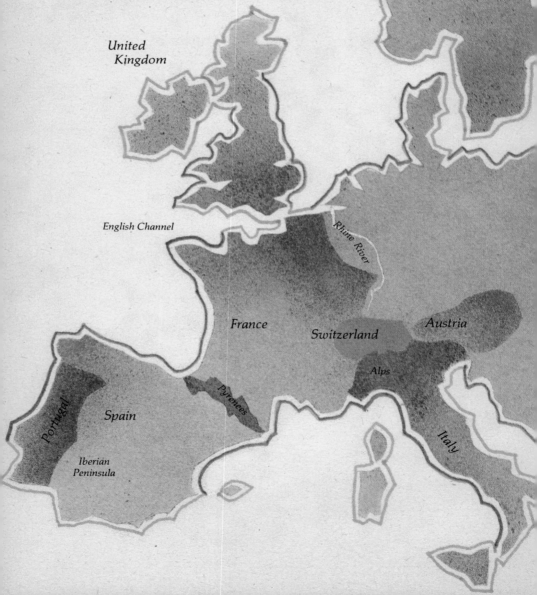

United Kingdom

English Channel

Rhine River

France

Switzerland

Austria

Alps

Portugal

Spain

Pyrenees

Italy

Iberian Peninsula

The jagged mountain range called the Alps separates Italy from France, Switzerland, and Austria. A narrow waterway called the English Channel separates the British Isles from the rest of the continent. And the Rhine River forms part of the border between France and Germany.

Language, customs, and traditions also separate the countries of Europe. Portugal and Spain make up the section of Europe called the Iberian Peninsula. There are no natural borders between these countries. But their peoples speak different languages, and their governments have followed different paths for many centuries.

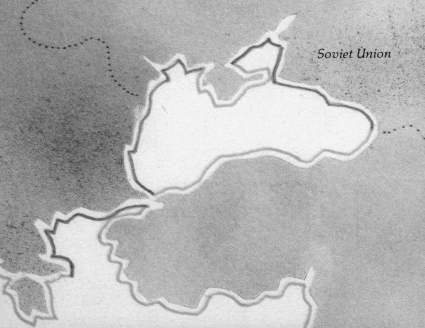

Soviet Union

Language is the main factor that separates Romania from the surrounding countries of Bulgaria, Yugoslavia, Hungary, and the Soviet Union. The people in those surrounding countries speak Slavic languages, while Romanian is a Romance language that is related to French, Spanish, and Italian. The Romance languages developed from the language spoken by the ancient Romans. The word *Romania* itself comes from the word "Roman."

While there are many differences between the countries of Europe, there are also many similarities. For example, all five Scandinavian countries of Northern Europe have the same climate. These countries—Norway, Sweden, Denmark, Iceland, and Finland—have long, cold winters and short, cool summers.

All of them have large fishing industries and dairy farms. The climate of most of Western Europe is cool and moist because of winds that blow off the Atlantic Ocean.

These winds bring rain and moderate temperatures to Great Britain, France, Belgium, Germany, and the Netherlands. Winters in these countries are seldom very cold, and summers are seldom very hot. But farther inland, far from the ocean, temperatures are more extreme.

Fishing is a major industry in every European country that has a coastline. In much of Europe, farming and raising sheep and cattle are also important to the economy.

Farming in Europe is particularly productive. Although the same land has been farmed for centuries, the crops are abundant because of wise agricultural methods and a favorable climate.

Southern Europe enjoys a mild climate, with cool, wet winters and warm, dry summers. The Southern European countries of Spain, Portugal, Italy, Greece, and Yugoslavia export fruits and vegetables to countries all over the world. And like their Northern European neighbors, they have large fishing fleets.

The rivers of Europe are widely used for shipping manufactured goods and farm produce. Europe's rivers have always been important to the life and economy of the continent. Long before there were railroads or highways, the main avenues of transport and travel were rivers such as the Thames in Great Britain, the Rhine in Western Europe, and the Danube of Eastern Europe.

Today, along with its network of rivers and canals, Europe has a vast railroad system, a large number of modern roads and highways, and many airports. Just about every place in Europe can be reached without trouble from any other place on the continent.

Because European travel is uncomplicated, there is a great deal of trade among the nations. The Western European countries are linked together in an organization called the Common Market.

Under Common Market rules, it is simple for French people to buy German cars, for Norwegians to buy Spanish oranges, for Britons to buy French iron, and for Italians to buy Danish butter. By simplifying trade, the Common Market has done a lot to reduce the tensions that caused wars in Europe over hundreds of years.

No single European country produces everything it needs. So trade is necessary and important for every country in Europe.

Common Market members: Belgium, Denmark, France, West Germany, Greece, Ireland, Italy, Luxembourg, Netherlands, United Kingdom

Mining and industrial production are also important to the economic strength of Europe. Great quantities of coal are mined in Great Britain, France, Belgium, Germany, and in Eastern Europe. Iron ore is found in Sweden, France, and a number of other Western European countries. The Soviet Union also mines iron, nickel, copper, and many other metals.

Until recently, most of the oil used in Europe was imported from other parts of the world. But now the Soviet Union produces most of the oil it needs, and the Western European countries are beginning to tap the oil reserves that lie beneath the North Sea.

European industry turns out a wide variety of well-made products. Swiss watches, British woolens, German and French cars, and Swedish steel are world famous.

Many of the people of Europe are skilled workers, who are also well educated. Every country on the continent has free public schools and fine universities. Only a small percentage of Europeans cannot read and write.

Most of the people of Europe also enjoy a decent standard of living, good housing, and medical care. And every European country is rich in museums, libraries, concert halls, opera houses, and historical landmarks.

Over the centuries Europe has given the world great writers, such as Shakespeare, Dante, Tolstoy, and Goethe; great artists, such as da Vinci, Rembrandt, Picasso, and van Gogh; and great composers, such as Beethoven, Bach, Mozart, and Verdi.

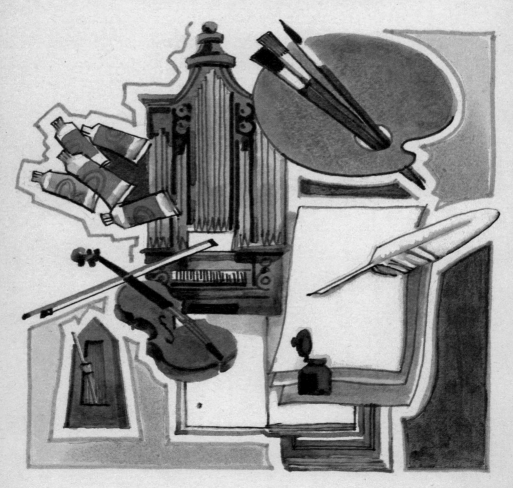

Europe's cities stand as symbols of ideas and culture. There is Athens, the capital of Greece, with its ruins of the ancient Parthenon; Rome, site of the Colosseum and the magnificent Vatican City; Paris, home of the Cathedral of Notre Dame; London, with its stately houses of Parliament and Buckingham Palace; and Madrid, with its handsome, treasure-filled Prado Museum.

But the cities of Europe are more than storehouses of its glorious past. They are vital nerve centers with large populations, modern buildings, and high-speed transportation. And the countrysides are more than old castles and ancient monuments. They are highly productive agricultural and industrial communities. If anything, time has made the continent of Europe even stronger and more exciting than ever.